Encyclopedia Of Spiritual Development

Book Four

Pam Brittan

Encyclopedia of Spirit original copyright Pam Brittan 2013

Website: www.spiritenergyuk.co.uk

Email: pambrittan@spiritenergyuk.co.uk

DEDICATION

I dedicate this to all my family and friends and those who have supported me through my many years of working with Spirit.
Most of all I am humbled by the messages I have received from those in the Spirit World to enable me to collate this book for sale.

This forth encyclopedia endeavors to complete the knowledge of Mental Mediumship and show how our links are called perception, which is another word for clairvoyant abilities.

The Chapter on Physical Mediumship covers a range of physical phenomena that can sometimes occur during our connection with the Spirit World.

We can only be in wonder of how the Spirit World can produce such spectacles; but when this is seen it can be awe inspiring and even a little daunting.

In today's fast pace of the world we can see that the development of certain aspects of this phenomena has sparked a media interest in all "ghostly" happenings.

Is this co-incidental? Not at all, We need to see and hear more. Spirit needs to get noticed by a wider audience and to bring about the belief that there is more than what we can physically see and hear!

CONTENTS

Chapter 1: Mental Mediumship:

Perception and Control

Chapter 2: Physical Mediumship:

Apports

Ectoplasm

Materialization

Transfiguration

Percussion

Levitation

Direct Voice

Independent Voice

Slate Writing

Spirit Painting

This book tells of the different types of Mediumship, Mental and Physical . Although I have not put practice sessions within this book you should still practice with others to develop your gift. Physical Mediumship is very much for the trained and developed Medium who has sat for trance and feels the time is right for them to sit for this type of phenomena. However to understand about this will help you to recognize when you have reached the level needed for this expertise.

Look for a circle you can attend, make sure that it is run by a competent medium who has experience. You need to feel safe in their hands!!!!!!

Spiritual development takes as long as it takes, I always say trust those teachers and helpers in the Spirit World because they will know when you are ready for the next part of your journey. There are times when we are stopped from going in a direction we thought was the right one, this is because, either we are not as ready as we think we are or it is not the way you are supposed to go. Taking the path is only the first step to a very long journey. Spirit has led me all the way. Obstacles are there for a reason, Just ACCEPT.

Often I see people with good intentions begin to lose their way because their thoughts are only what they can get out of it and not for the higher good for all. In the last couple of years I have had to take a step back and re-assess, this is when I was inspired to produce these books.

So everything has a reason, and I've learnt to take all things as they are and not what I want them to be.

Work with the joy of your spirit,

And be true to yourself and to them!

Chapter One

Mental Mediumship – Perception and Control

WHAT IS A MEDIUM?

Mediums are ordinary people who have developed their natural abilities to communicate with the Spirit World.

WHAT THEN IS A PSYCHIC?

These are ordinary people who have developed their extrasensory, telepathic abilities to communicate with their fellow human beings.

BOTH GIFTS CONNECT TO PROVIDE A PERSON WITH THE ABILITY NOT ONLY TO CONNECT WITH THE SPIRIT WORLD BUT WITH "SPIRIT BEINGS WALKING ON THE EARTH"

In this way they will gather information from someone in the Spirit World and relay it to someone here. Usually it is someone connected in some way to the recipient. This is done either in a public demonstration, in a church service, or as a private sitting where more detail can be given.

THERE ARE THREE MAIN TYPES OF MEDIUMSHIP

Mental   **Healing**   **Physical**

As discussed Healing can be part of Mental Mediumship, as well as Physical Mediumship Healing with the Physical is trance healing which will be explained in a later book.

Perception

The main purpose of mediumship is to provide evidence of survival. The most common way this is done is through this type of mediumship, *perception.*

The medium perceives information through their psychic senses, the general term is clairvoyance.

However, Spiritualist mediums use the term **clairvoyance** in a more specific way (clear-seeing), for they also use the terms **clairaudience** (hearing) and **clairsentience** (sensing or feeling).

It must be accepted that we cannot prove life after death scientifically as yet! What we can do is provide enough evidence so that the individual will have no doubts about the proof given.

By communicating with someone in the Spirit World a medium can pass on a sufficient amount of information about them to provide that evidence. The Medium's job is to identify who communicates with them, why they have come and what is the message.

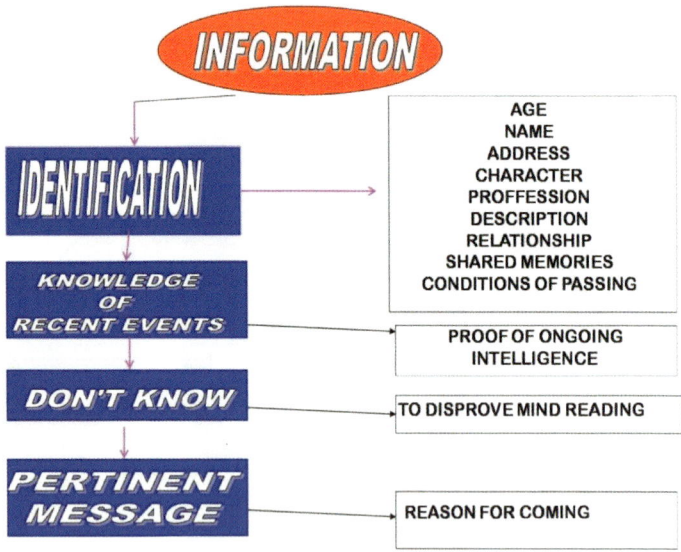

The medium needs to establish enough information about the deceased before they died, for instance what their character was like, something pertinent to them maybe they made dresses or were a carpenter, etc...

The next bit of information should include some events that have happened since they died. We call this 'knowledge of recent events' and it gives us proof of ongoing existence

If you already know all of the information that has been given, then it could have come from your own mind, and again does not prove life after death.

There needs to be a piece of information that you do not know the answer to. If you then research it and find out that it is also true, it provides further evidence.

To complete our communication there also needs to be a pertinent message, or reason for coming. This may simply be to say "I love you", or could be something far more detailed.

When you have all of the above elements in place we have to ask ourselves "what is the most likely single source of all of this information?" Spiritualists hold it to be from those we have known who have survived the event called death and simply want to tell us so.

The message can come objectively which is actually seeing or hearing in the physical sense

If we obtain the message subjectively then this comes through the mind and the "third eye"

We access this information within our brow chakra, we communicate with our throat chakra (see Book One). At this stage I have a saying:

DON'T THINK JUST LINK

As thoughts come into your head do not try to analyse this information. This is a time when you must accept the facts and express your thoughts.

Another saying I have is:

DON'T DOUBT GIVE OUT

So it is better at first not to think too much about what it is you are getting, remember, it may not make sense to you, but to the person on the receiving end it will have a profound meaning.

In my early days of serving the churches I had a old fashioned horse drawn gypsy caravan given to me, and, instead of giving just that, I tried to put my own interpretation to it by saying "Someone in the family must connect with the old fashion gypsies"

The gentleman who was in receipt of this message immediately said no that is not right, but, bless him, because we were just training he helped me by telling me his father who I had established was the man who had come through, was a carpenter and he had made a miniature version of this gypsy caravan with a horse when he was a boy. and he still has it and he wanted to pass it on to his grandson.

So you can see, if I had just explained what I had got and not tried to create my own version, the gentleman would have completely understood.

As we "receive" this information, we need to ask the Spirit Link questions within our head. Remember, this is in the imaginative part of the Brain so we must **TRUST** what we are getting. So our first question is "Who are you?"

Sometimes you will get a specific name, often, we get told I am Dad, or Mum. You have then to establish where the link goes, certainly this is important at a public venue, if it is one to one then this link is already recognized.

I have often said during this time I would love to have Name, Address and Telephone Number!!!! But, you can get as much information as you can during this time—what their personality was like, shared memories, description of them, maybe where they lived (this may not include their address but a description of their home how it looked etc).

As you work with this link, your only source of information is this link; so keep going back until you have gathered as much as you can.

Then you can bring the Spirit Link to relay some ongoing event. Often, this will reveal there is a birthday, anniversary, thinking about someone who is ill. During this connection you are given some knowledge that the recipient may not know and will have to go home and research—this has many advantages in that often this information can only have come from that particular person who has gone to the Spirit World.

You must then try to relay the message and the reason they have made such a big effort to connect with the person.

Responsibility has to be foremost in how you portray the link. For instance, if a Father has come through and he smoked and drank all his life and didn't much connect with his family, remember, you do not have to judge that situation you are only the "telephone" link and must give the message in a diplomatic way to inspire rather than despair the recipient.

If you see a rather large lady, it would be so much more discreet to say "I have a rounded lady, here rather than a big fat lady"

Words can be very hurtful so be responsible with how you use them.

Remember, also these are loved ones who have come to speak or make peace with those here on the earth plane.

We talk about the World Wide Web then think of this as "Wonderful, Wisdom, and Worthwhile"

Control

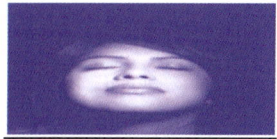

Control mediumship is more commonly known as trance mediumship. The medium has the ability to allow the mind of a Spirit person to blend with their own to such an extent that they can assume a certain degree of control over the medium.

As this is through the mind, the medium will always to some degree influence what takes place.

It is easier for the Spirit control to use what is there than to bring through something that is completely original. It is only with the more developed trance mediums that this takes place.

We can allow the Spirit people to control us for a number of different purposes: healing, speaking, writing, painting or for the production of physical phenomena.

Speaking

Speaking or allowing a Spirit control to speak through us whilst in the trance state gives access to divine inspiration on an ongoing basis. Over the last 150+ years we have had an immense amount of philosophy, guidance and encouragement from those that love us and want to help us to live more spiritual lives.

Writing

Writing whilst being controlled is called automatic writing. The Spirit author controls the mediums hand to write, sometimes in their own handwriting, or in mirror writing. It is possible for the more developed automatic writing, that Mediums will have both hands simultaneously writing. In mirror writing by two different Spirit controls.

Painting

Painting in the trance state is similar to writing in that the hands are controlled. The end result can be quite spectacular in that pictures in the style of the great masters can be produced with great speed.

Also it is possible when Psychic Artists use this ability to produce a picture of a loved one in the Spirit World as well as bringing a message from them.

At the beginning of Chapter Two is a diagram that sets out the effect of physical mediumship on the system e.g. nervous, mental, emotional etc.

The diagram explains different aspects of the physical mediumship which I will explain as the reader approaches each section.

No doubt, there will be several of these physical phenomena which you have experienced—light touches and spirit light for instance.

I call these lights twinkles and the touches can be so light we think it's our imagination, but, how many of you have experienced someone touching your hair or cheek.

Chapter Eleven

Physical Mediumship

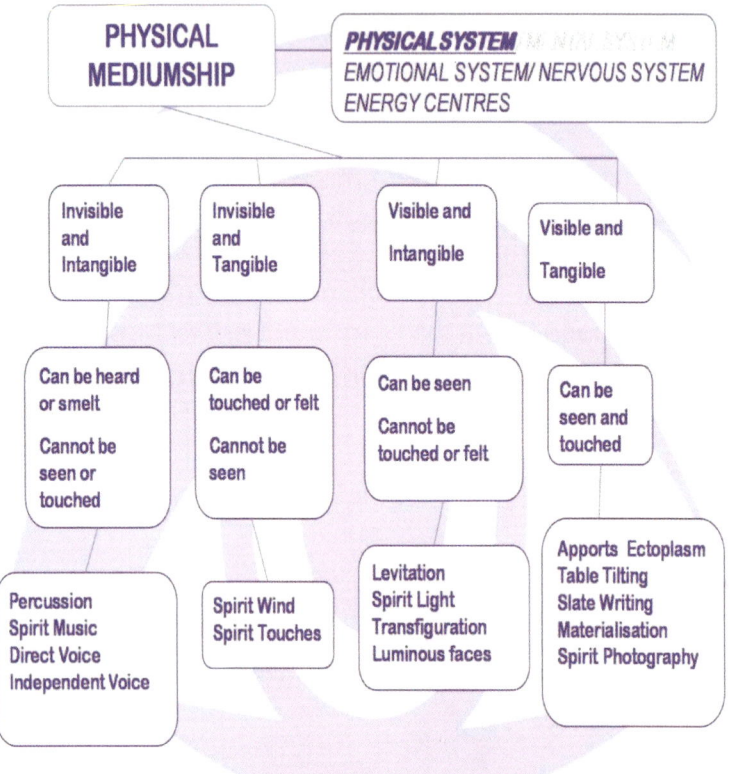

Spiritualism was founded upon physical mediumship. In 1848 two young girls, who later became world famous physical mediums, who established communication with the spirit of a murdered peddler. They were **Margaret and Kate Fox**, they did this by establishing a code via rapping's, or what is technically called percussion.

This event that took place at Hydesville in New York State, USA, and it was a breakthrough. It established that not only does the human personality survive death, but under the right conditions it is possible to communicate. From that moment onwards there was an explosion of physical phenomena right across North America, finally reaching England in 1852.

Hydesville

For any kind of phenomena to be categorised as physical it must impinge upon one or more of the five physical senses, i.e... You must be able to see it, hear it or feel it etc. and everyone present will witness the same event.

Over the 150 plus years since Hydesville there has been a vast array of phenomena produced by the Spirit world.

Apports

An apport is a physical object that has been dematerialised in one location, transported to another and re-materialised. The two pictures are the front and back of an apport that was materialised at Stansted Hall in April 2002 through the mediumship of Minister Judith Seaman. It measures about 2½ inches square, and is made from card. It was a "present" for one of the Italian students from her sister in the Spirit world.

I often make my students laugh because they are all in awe of the phenomena and are agog with what I am talking about then I break the intense atmosphere by stating (tongue in cheek) "and on the postcard was Wish you were here"

Joking aside what magnificent proof of life eternal can we have than a physical article placed in our hands

In the previous week, under similar conditions a feather was apported. The unusual feature of the feather was its incredibly strong perfume.

These apports were produced by one of Judith's spirit controls, called Amy; she called forward the recipient from the audience, extended Judith's hand palm down, and as the recipient placed their hand beneath, it simply appeared there.

Ectoplasm

Ectoplasm is a substance taken from the mediums body and according to Arthur Findlay, mixed with an etheric substance. This enables the spirit controls to affect physical matter.

Depending upon the way it was developed it is very often light sensitive. For that reason many séances are held in either total darkness or a low red light.

Ectoplasm is extruded from the medium through any opening, very often through the mouth, ears or nostrils. The picture shows Jack Webber with ectoplasm streaming from his mouth.

In 1990 when a séance was held with Gordon Higginson at Stansted Hall ectoplasm started to come from the solar plexus area as a thin cloud.

It then condensed and formed into two arms complete with hands.

This phenomena would come from dedication on behalf of the medium and those who would sit for them. Years ago before the advent of TV many people would run home Circles.

A circle is people who come together to sit with a experienced medium for various reasons.

It can be for their own development or for the development of the Medium to create phenomena as we see in evidence in the picture showing the ectoplasm.

Gordon Higginson

The picture shows an Ectoplasmic rod about to levitate a table

Ectoplasmic phenomena are now very rare. One of the reasons for this is; it takes a very long time it to develop. It can also be quite hazardous for the medium.

On several occasions the physical medium Helen Duncan had her séances raided by the police to try to prove fraud. When they tried to grab hold of the materialised forms the ectoplasm withdrew so rapidly back into her that it caused internal haemorrhaging.

Hence the security of closed doors during trance meetings. Great care is taken when these are open to public demonstrations.

Helen Duncan

She died of heart failure ten days after her last séance was disrupted like this. Hence today if séances are used for these phenomena there is an emphasis on safety of the medium. Security is paramount so these séances are often held within enclosed premises with only invited people to attend.

Materialisation

This is probably the most astonishing of all physical phenomena. Although having said that, most of the leading investigators have agreed that the best evidence of survival was obtained through voice phenomena, as they could hold lengthy conversations with the spirit people.

The picture shows the materialised form of Katie King, the medium was Florence Cook. Sir William Crookes was not only allowed to photograph and examine her, he was even allowed to cut a lock of her hair.

This lock of hair is currently owned by the SNU and is kept in their museum at Stansted Hall, Arthur Findlay College.

Transfiguration

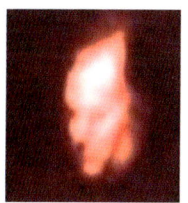

A transfiguration medium has a 'mask' of ectoplasm formed over or just in front of their face. This then moulds into the face of a spirit person which can be recognized by someone present.

I have seen this happen, again, during a stay at the Arthur Findlay College, a group of us from our Church attended a meeting showing a Transfiguration Medium in action.

I remember saying to my friend that she was to have a brilliant experience this particular week. But, so far, this had not proved right.

We all sat in amazement at the mask building up and the voice of the Medium. Then the Medium called my friend's name and asked her to step forward.

Her Mother appeared and spoke to her which was so intense she began to cry. This had an impact on all of us because the information was so profound.

Everyone from the Church shed a tear and to this day I will always have that fantastic memory of real proof of survival.

Percussion

Percussion, or as it is commonly known as raps, is how it all started in 1848. Raps or knockings can be clearly heard from any point in the room. Crawford who investigated Kathleen Golliger, stated that raps would vary in intensity and volume from very quiet taps right up to "sledge hammer like blows" that could be heard out in the street.

By establishing a code, for example one rap for "Yes" and two for "No" it is possible to ask questions. In a similar way it can happen with a bedside lamp, or any objects that can produce the required code.

To establish this code you need to ask basic questions by establishing a response to your questions.

Progressing on from this simple code you can then try the full alphabet to get more detailed answers. You start reciting the alphabet, "A, B, C..." etc. and when you get to the letter they require they rap.

As you can imagine, this is very slow and laborious. Communication this way has its uses but I can see why it was essential to progress onto more speedy ways. But, it all had to start somewhere and this is the simplest and easiest to develop.

I have a little tale to tell during renovations to my house we had to have the whole place rewired.

The electrician came to finish off towards the end and my kitchen light kept flashing. He checked in the loft and the wiring but nothing at all was wrong. I said "I know who is doing that, my husband's Granddad " he would often come to visit and he would let us know he was there.

I said to the electrician "Watch this, two flashes for yes, one for no, is that you Granddad" the light flashed twice.

The electrician quickly drank his tea and said "I'm out of here" and left in a rush. So you can see we can all experience this sort of phenomena.

Levitation

Levitation is the movement of objects without normal means of support.

This can be done by either psycho-kinetic energy (telekinesis) or by the use of ectoplasm. The picture shows a table in midair during a séance.

Probably the most amazing example of levitation was through the mediumship of D.D. Hume. On over 100 occasions during the 1860's and 1870's he was levitated up to the ceiling and often around the room above the heads of the sitters.

On one occasion he was levitated out the window of a third story room and in through the window of an adjacent room.

Can you imagine what Health and Safety would have to say if Mediums were to begin this today.!!! It takes a lot of effort for this to happen, and it is a rare phenomena today.

Direct Voice

For the spirit world to be able to speak to us using their own voice they have to able to vibrate the physical atmosphere. As they do not have a physical body they have to find an artificial way to do this.

One way is to create an artificial voice box out of ectoplasm this enables them to talk to us as they once did when they lived upon the earth.

Because the voice box can very often be small and very quiet, the assistance of a trumpet is often used to not only amplify the sound but also to direct to the person they wish to speak to.

A séance trumpet is a cone of aluminium or card about 2 feet long (60cms) by spirit making the voice box in the small end it will act as a simple megaphone and amplify the sounds.

In the picture the ectoplasm is coming out of one of his ears to produce a voice box for direct voice phenomena.

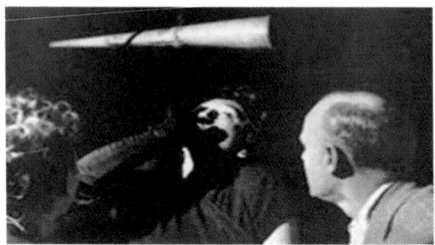

Independent voice

Independent voice phenomena differ from direct voice in that it is not connected to the medium by way of an Ectoplasmic rod; also a trumpet is not required. Voices are simply heard as if coming from midair and can be from any point in the room.

One of the most powerful voice mediums was Etta Wreight. She came from the USA to England in 1913 to demonstrate her mediumship.

At some of her séances she had up to three trumpets and independent voice operating simultaneously. Records of these séances are contained in the book 'The Voices' by Vice-Admiral Usbourne Moore.

There have been reports of "Independent Voice" coming through speakers at home or even on Tape Recordings.

I used to tape my sittings with clients and on one such occasion, I had the young girl's grandfather who wanted to tell her that he was OK and that her mum shouldn't worry.

When the client played the tape at home for her mum, a voice on the tape clearly said her name. This was not audible in the room so I would not like to say which phenomena this was but the effect was just overwhelming for both mother and daughter, and it proves Spirit will always find a way of getting in touch!

Slate Writing

Two miniature blackboards that were used by school children were joined together by hinges. This enabled them to be closed like a book. A minute piece of chalk could then be placed in the cavity that is formed in the middle; it would then be bound and sealed.

The medium would hold the sealed slates in his hand; the lights turned out and after a few minutes back on.

When the slates were unsealed and opened there would be writing on the boards in the hand of whoever was communicating.

Some examples of these slates can be seen in the SNU museum at Stansted Hall, Arthur Findlay College.

Spirit Painting

David Duguid, a Scottish medium, had a remarkable gift for creating spirit paintings. He could hold a small card, sometimes only measuring 4" x 3" (100mm x 50mm), between his hands and in less than two minutes a small but very detailed picture would be produced.

Spirit Photography

During the explanations of Physical Phenomena I have not explained about Spirit Photography. Spirit can often appear on photographs taken randomly with a digital camera, sometimes you may see a mist appear in front of someone or behind them. This is definitely a buildup of Spirit.

I have had reports of wedding group photos where "Auntie Maud" has appeared in the photo when she has in fact been gone to the Spirit World for years.

When I attended a course at Arthur Findlay College we did an experiment with "Scotography" in essence we had a piece of blank photographic paper put on our laps and went into meditation, they were then developed, in theory the paper should have been black, but each person could recognize something.

There was colour and my husband had a side profile of his son who died at the age of 12. So you can see in today's technology we can capture Spirit more and more.

Spirit Music, Light and Touch

Spirit Music can be heard every now and again it seems to come from nowhere and seems ethereal; I have never experienced this but know of others who have.

The sound may appear faintly but people can be very aware of it, it may sound like Santa's Sleigh Bells.

As I have explained earlier Spirit Light is like twinkles or globes of light. Twinkling on and off randomly. I sat in circle with some good friends of mine and we all saw a globe of light come into the room and then go out once the Medium had finished their trance.

Sometimes the light is not so pronounced but just a small light that catches you from the corner of your eye.

The touches can come when we least expect it, you may feel your hair being moved, a cobweb seemingly going over your face.

When this happens don't just dismiss it, it is often a reassurance from your loved ones that they are near and thinking of you.

Physical Phenomena can be felt and seen by us all. If you get the chance to attend a Trance Demonstration it would be very worthwhile.

Not only would you gain more knowledge but you would be able then to judge whether this is the route you wish to take. Some aspects of these phenomena may not be readily available until we are more experienced and ready for that next step. Indeed, there are very few Physical Mediums now in circulation.

As time has gone on maybe, Spirit are finding more up to date methods of enabling communication between us. Do not dismiss anything; it is NOT just your imagination.

There is more to other dimensions than we know. My aim with these books is to make it less mysterious and available to all people.

You can ask why Physical Phenomena does not happen so much today, that is because we have less patience and want everything to happen yesterday.

Spirit are finding more amenable ways of getting their message to us. There is a curiosity that I haven't seen in many years, more youngsters are becoming spiritually aware which is wonderful. We hear of so much negativity maybe, this is the start of a new chapter and a shift of consciousness for the coming of years.

Looking forward and not back has to be the answer.

Spiritually we have more growth to make, none of us will ever know everything, but, the fascination and enthrall it has had for me over the many years of my learning and evolvement has changed my perception so much.

I will never lecture anyone to believe but I ask you to research, learn, and ACCEPT. *Which will only come when you are ready.*

I often say knowledge is power, but sometimes being naive and coming to something completely raw can add an excitement to a subject as well as a new perception to the tutor.

Often in the teaching we can learn; I never take it as read that I KNOW EVERYTHING because, dear reader, that would be very stupid of me!!!!!!

Even with all the experience during my many years of Mediumship I am still in awe of the messages, the synchronicity and the co-incidences that happen to enable us to be where we are, who we are with, and doing what we are doing.

No matter how old or experienced we think we have become, nothing can prepare us for the wonderful way Spirit can show us the way.

Oscar Wilde said "Life is far too important a thing ever to talk seriously about "

Live life and let Spirit guide you

Love and light

Pam Brittan

Book Five:
Trance
Power Animals
Higher Consciousness

Printed in Great Britain
by Amazon.co.uk, Ltd.,
Marston Gate.